BODY SENSE, BODY NONSENSE

Seymour Simon
Illustrated by Dennis Kendrick

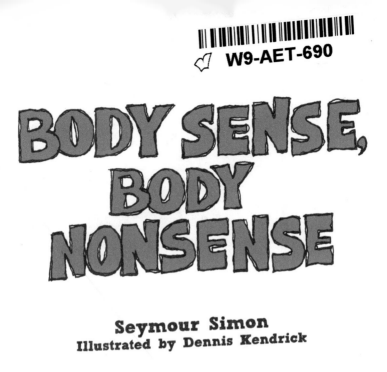

DOVER PUBLICATIONS, INC.
Mineola, New York

For my sisters
Miriam and Roslyn
from their kid brother

Bibliographical Note

Body Sense, Body Nonsense, first published by Dover Publications, Inc., in
2012, is an unabridged republication of the work published by J.B. Lippincott
Junior Books, New York, in 1981.

International Standard Book Number

ISBN-13: 978-0-486-48528-7
ISBN-10: 0-486-48528-5

Manufactured in the United States by Courier Corporation
48528502
www.doverpublications.com

INTRODUCTION

Does eating pickles and ice cream make you sick? Does eating spinach make you strong? Should you go swimming right after you eat? There are many stories and sayings about your body that you may have heard. But do you know which ones make sense? Or which ones are nonsense?

Even if you think some story makes sense, it is not always easy to be sure. For example, you may feel sick if you eat pickles and ice cream, but someone else may not be bothered.

In this book, we'll look at some common sayings about your body. Think about whether each saying is sense or nonsense. Then turn the page to find out if you are right. You'll also find out the reasons why scientists and doctors think the saying is true or false.

SEYMOUR SIMON, whom the *New York Times* called "the dean of [children's science] writers," is the author of more than 250 highly acclaimed science books. He has introduced tens of millions of children to a staggering array of subjects in his books, which encourage young people to enjoy the world around them through learning and discovery, and by making science fun. Simon taught science and creative writing in elementary and secondary schools and was chair of the science department at a junior high school in the New York City public school system before leaving to become a full-time writer. "I haven't really given up teaching," he says, "and I suppose I never will, not as long as I keep writing and talking to kids around the country and the world."

AN APPLE A DAY KEEPS THE DOCTOR AWAY ?

NONSENSE

An apple a day will only keep the doctor away if you throw it at him. Eating apples will not prevent you from becoming sick or help you get better if you are sick.

Eating apples to become healthy is an idea that dates back hundreds of years. In Roman times, no feast was complete without apples. An old rhyme states, "Eat an apple before going to bed,/Makes the doctor beg his bread." In folk tales, there are many magical charms based on the apple.

Of course, eating apples is not all nonsense. For most people, an apple can be a healthy part of a meal. It contains small amounts of vitamins and minerals. But even more important, an apple contains a good amount of crude plant fiber. The fiber provides bulk and helps your digestive system to work well. So maybe eating an apple a day isn't such a bad idea after all.

COUNTING SHEEP HELPS PUT YOU TO SLEEP ?

3

SENSE

Counting sheep jumping over a fence seems to be one of the sillier ways of trying to fall asleep. But some experiments have shown that it really seems to work. Of course, if you don't like sheep you can count horses, dogs, or any other animal that appeals to you. The trick is to keep your brain so busy with a boring task, that you don't have time to worry about other things.

Here's why. Thinking about an animal occupies the right side of your brain. That prevents it from coming up with other images that might disturb you. Counting, which is a different kind of mental activity, takes place in the left side of your brain. The counting prevents you from concentrating on other problems that might keep you awake trying to solve them.

So counting sheep as they jump over a fence (or dance across a field) keeps both sides of your brain busy, and that lets you fall asleep more easily. Why don't you try it and see what happens.

NONSENSE

A black eye is a bruise. When a hard object (such as a fist!) comes in contact with someone's eye, it may break small blood vessels just beneath the surface of the skin. The bleeding darkens or blackens the eye.

Sometimes you can prevent the bleeding by immediately pressing something cold against the eye. The cold tightens the blood vessels and stops the blood from flowing out.

A cold, raw steak could be used to treat a black eye. But it's awfully expensive and not the best thing to use anyway. Some ice wrapped in a towel works better and doesn't cost nearly as much. Apply the ice for five minutes on and five minutes off.

Once the eye has blackened, neither ice nor a steak will help. The bruise will clear up by itself in a few days. Of course, you can always broil the steak and make yourself feel better that way.

TREAT A BURN WITH BUTTER ?

NONSENSE

Any large burn needs to be seen by a doctor as soon as possible. Any small burn that blisters or breaks the skin should also be treated by a doctor. Placing butter on a bad burn is not a good idea. Butter kept in your refrigerator is not sterile; it may contain germs. The butter won't prevent scarring and may even infect the burn.

The best first-aid treatment for a small burn is to place the burned area in cold water (but not on ice). Keep it there for a while. You can keep a burn in cold water for an hour if necessary. The cold water will soothe the pain and will help prevent scars. You can also apply a sterile burn cream or ointment to a small burn.

The best thing to do with a bad burn is get a doctor immediately. Don't do anything at all to the burned area. The victim should lie down and be kept quiet until the doctor comes.

The note reads: "Puss— Went to see Dr. Patchum— Back soon. Hold all my calls. Mumsy"

HOLDING YOUR BREATH CAN CURE HICCUPS ?

SENSE

Lots of things may cure an attack of hiccups. You can try holding your breath for as long as you can. You can also try breathing the air in a paper bag for a few minutes. These methods make you rebreathe the carbon-dioxide gas that you normally exhale.

The build-up of carbon dioxide in your lungs and blood sends a signal to your brain. Your brain sends out a signal to your diaphragm muscles. You begin to breathe more deeply. The deep breathing movements will usually break the pattern of hiccups.

The diaphragm is the large muscle that separates your chest from your abdomen. Hiccups can be caused by anything that disturbs the nerves that go to the diaphragm. Eating very hot foods, swallowing air, or even talking while eating are just some things that can cause you to get hiccups.

Here are some other simple ways to cure hiccups. Slowly sip a glass or two of cold water. Tickle your nose so that you will sneeze. Pull on your tongue. All these methods stimulate a nerve at the back of your mouth and may end your hiccups.

I JUST TRIED THE TICKLE-YOUR-NOSE CURE...

DID IT CURE YOUR HICCUPS?

SURE, BUT NOW I CAN'T S-STOP...AH-**AH**-ᑕᕼOO!

REDHEADS HAVE BAD TEMPERS ?

NONSENSE

Some redheads do have bad tempers. But some redheads don't. Just like with people of other hair colors, it depends upon the individual.

But it's easier to tell when a redhead gets angry than when a dark-haired person gets angry. Here's why. When a person gets angry or excited, little blood vessels under the skin enlarge and fill with blood. We say that a person "flushes."

If you have dark hair and a dark skin, the flush is very faint. But redheads usually have a pale skin. The blood vessels show through more readily. When redheads flush, their faces become fiery red.

People may not even notice the flush on a dark-haired person. But they may think that the redhead is very angry because of the red face. That makes them think that all redheads have a terrible temper.

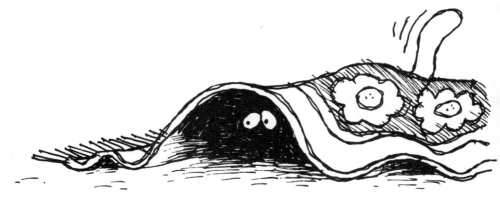

BRUSH YOUR HAIR ONE HUNDRED TIMES EACH NIGHT

NONSENSE

Brushing your hair does make it shinier. But brushing also pulls out hair and splits the ends. You're much better off just brushing your hair enough to keep it neat. If you want your hair to be shinier, just massage your scalp with your fingertips.

Also, it's not a good idea to brush or pull at your hair when it's wet. Hair is not as strong and springy when it is wet. It may break or be pulled out with even a slight pull. Just pat your wet hair into place and wait until it dries before you comb or brush it.

Your hair is dead tissue. But it grows from living roots in your scalp. Your scalp also has many tiny oil glands. It's the oil from these glands that makes your hair shiny. Too much brushing or rubbing may make your hair and skin too oily.

Sometimes when you become sick, the glands dry up. Your hair becomes brittle and dull. But when you get well, the oil glands begin to work and your hair looks shiny again.

DRAFTS CAUSE COLDS ?

NONSENSE

Colds are not caused by drafts, by going out in cold weather, or by getting your feet wet. Colds are caused by only one thing. You catch a cold from someone who already has a cold. The cause is a cold virus, which is passed on from person to person.

Someone who has a cold sneezes and coughs. That scatters cold viruses into the air. Breathing in the viruses is what causes a cold in the next person. Even talking to a person with a cold can cause you to catch a cold yourself.

Cold viruses can also be carried by handkerchiefs, eating utensils, and almost any object handled by a person with a cold. The virus can be picked up from the throat and spread by hand. That's one good reason to wash your hands to prevent spreading germs. Colds are most catching in the first day or two.

Of course, other things around you can *help* you to catch a cold. Your ability to resist catching a cold can be weakened if you are over-tired, ill-fed, or sick for some other reason. Sudden changes in the weather, or going from a heated room to the cold outdoors and then back again, also seem to lower your resistance.

SENSE

A full moon may not drive people mad, but people seem to do strange things at that time. Police records often show an increase in crimes when the moon is full. There was even a recent study of murders over a fifteen-year period in a large city. The study showed that there were more murders during the time of the new moon and full moon than at any other time of the month.

History is full of stories and legends about the full moon. Perhaps the most famous is the legend of the werewolf, a person who changes into a wolf in the light of the full moon. Of course, there is no truth to that, but the word lunatic itself comes from the Latin word *luna*, which means moon.

Even if people do act strangely when there is a full moon, no one knows exactly why. The moon's gravitational pull does cause tides. And the time of the highest and lowest tides occurs at full and new moon.

Many animals behave in different ways at the time of these tides. Perhaps some people are also influenced in some of the things they do by the gravitational pull of the full moon.

$$3 + 2\left(y^2 - b\right) = 927$$

$$5 \times \left(\sqrt{54}\right) + 3b-$$

$$\frac{2x + y}{y^3} = 4x+$$

NONSENSE

No one food is used by your brain or any other part of your body. It would be wonderful to become smarter just by eating fish. Most people would prefer to eat a tuna-fish sandwich rather than study. But sadly, you won't become any brainier from the tuna.

The idea that fish is brain food dates back to the last century. Scientists had just found a mineral called phosphorus in the brain. They also found that fish contained the same mineral. Some people connected the two ideas. They said that people need phosphorus to think, so eating fish would help you think.

But what these people didn't know was that phosphorus is found in most foods. So fish is no better for your brain than eggs, milk, meat, or cereal.

Foods contain materials called nutrients. Phosphorus is only one of many nutrients your body and brain need. Different foods may have different nutrients. So to get all the nutrients you need it's a good idea to eat a selection of different foods. That's what scientists call a balanced diet.

EATING PICKLES AND ICE CREAM MAKES YOU SICK

NONSENSE

You might get sick if you eat too many pickles or too much ice cream. But eating a pickle and some ice cream together will not make you ill—unless you don't like the combination. But if that's what you like, then enjoy your meal!

Pickles are a very acid food. Ice cream is made of milk (and other things). The idea behind the saying was that the acid in the pickles would curdle the milk in the ice cream. And, of course, you wouldn't want to eat curdled milk.

But the truth is that your stomach makes acid to help digest food. So even if you swallow fresh ice cream or milk, it will curdle in your stomach anyway, even without the pickles. The curdling of milk is just the first step in its digestion in your body.

BEES STING "SWEET" PEOPLE ？

SENSE

Have you ever been stung by a bee? Perhaps your mother or your father comforted you by saying that bees sting people that are "sweet." Well, your parents may have been right. You are more likely to be stung by a bee if you smell or taste sweet.

It seems that bees are attracted to ice cream, jam, and sticky sweet candies. If you eat these sweets out-of-doors, you may attract bees. In attempting to brush the bees away, you may get stung.

You may attract bees if you wear a perfume, or use a sweet-smelling lotion of some kind. Bees are also attracted to bright colors. So don't be surprised if a flowery print on a shirt or dress attracts a buzzing visitor.

It's a good idea to keep food on a picnic tightly covered until you eat. Also, wash your hands and face after eating so that all traces of sweet foods are gone. If you do get stung, just apply some cold water or ice or some burn ointment. See a doctor if the pain lasts long or if you begin to feel sick.

CHEW YOUR FOOD TWENTY TIMES BEFORE SWALLOWING

NONSENSE

You may have been told to chew your food twenty, fifty, or even one hundred times before you swallow. The idea was to break your food into very tiny bits so that you would get all the nutrients out. It may sound reasonable, but it doesn't work.

The food you eat is digested in your stomach and small intestine, not in your mouth. You can chew your food all day long, but unless you swallow it, the food won't do you any good.

The breakdown of food does begin in your mouth. Your saliva contains chemicals that begin to break up the food. But you can swallow a piece of food without chewing and get exactly the same benefit from the nutrients in the food.

That does not mean that you shouldn't chew your food or take small bites. A large piece of food can easily get stuck in your throat and choke you. So chew your food, but don't worry about counting the number of chews.

MMMMM!! THAT WAS **GREAT** CUSTARD!

CARROTS ARE GOOD FOR YOUR EYESIGHT ?

SENSE

People who cannot see well in dim light are said to suffer from night blindness. This is not very serious for most of us. But pilots and others who drive at night depend upon their nighttime vision. Here's why eating carrots helps protect people from night blindness.

Night blindness is sometimes caused by not getting enough vitamin A in your diet. Carrots are a good source of vitamin A. So eating carrots once in a while can supply the vitamin A needed to prevent night blindness.

Of course, carrots are not the only good source of vitamin A. Broccoli, cabbage, pumpkin, spinach, sweet potatoes, tomatoes, and apricots are other good sources. Eating any of these would give you enough vitamin A.

DAYDREAMING IS A WASTE OF TIME

NONSENSE

It might seem that a person is not doing anything worthwhile when he is daydreaming, but that's not true. Daydreams are much like the dreams that you have at night. Both day and night dreaming can help you in many ways.

Dreams are the mind's way of letting your imagination roam free. Dreams can help you solve problems that you may have on your mind. They can give you ideas that you might not otherwise think of.

Dreaming is very necessary. In experiments, scientists deliberately woke up people just as they began to dream. (The scientists could tell by their subjects' rapid eye movements.) This was done all through the night. The next day the subjects were nervous and irritable. This happened even though they got the normal amount of sleep during the night. When the subjects were allowed to sleep without interruption, they dreamed much more than normal.

Scientists have learned that dreaming is important and not a waste of time. So the next time someone tells you to stop daydreaming, just tell him that you are using your imagination.

NONSENSE

Some people have the idea that they shouldn't drink water or any other liquid while they're exercising or playing in a sport such as tennis, basketball, or football. They think that the water will bloat them up and make them slower.

But if you run around a lot or exercise hard, your body loses water very rapidly. This water has to be replaced. Particularly in hot weather, your body may lose so much water that you become dehydrated (the word means "without water").

A dehydrated person may feel sick and dizzy. He may faint and even become very ill unless his missing liquids are replaced. So the next time you play ball or run around, take a drink whenever you get thirsty.

SENSE

The color of a room can change the way you feel in all kinds of ways. A room done in blues can make you feel calm and relaxed. Even looking at a sheet of blue paper can calm you down. Experiments have shown that blue surroundings lower your heart rate and blood pressure and also slow your breathing.

Yellows, on the other hand, can make you feel more active and happier. Reds can make you feel warmer and even more active than yellows. Sometimes too much red can be disturbing and make you feel nervous. But wearing a red dress or shirt will certainly get you attention.

If yellows and reds are too bright they can give you a headache. Blues and "cooler" colors make you feel quiet, but they may also make you feel cold. Which kinds of colors would you want to have in your bedroom? Which in a playroom? Can you tell why?

NONSENSE

Popeye may eat spinach to become stronger, but it won't do very much for you. Supposedly, Popeye becomes strong because of the iron in spinach. There is some iron in spinach, but not all that much.

Your body cannot even take in all of the small amount of iron in spinach. To get all the iron you need from spinach alone, you would have to eat your own weight in spinach every day. And that much spinach is not good for you for other reasons, even if you could eat it all.

You do need to take in iron to be healthy. Iron is used by your body to produce red blood cells. The best sources of iron in your diet are lean meats, liver, whole-grain cereals, and enriched breads.

NONSENSE

Eating sugary foods such as candy does increase the chance of your getting cavities in your teeth. The sugar encourages the growth of bacteria in your mouth. The bacteria and the sugar increase the amount of acid in your mouth. Acids eat away at your teeth and cause cavities.

But chewing gum seems to have a different effect. Even the small amount of sugar in some gum leaves your mouth very quickly. Chewing gum makes more saliva in your mouth. Saliva keeps your mouth neutral, rather than acid, so bacteria don't grow as easily.

Also, saliva may even strengthen your teeth. When you first get a tooth, it is very soft. Some of the minerals in saliva help the tooth to harden. More saliva means more minerals. So chewing gum not only doesn't give you cavities, it may even be good for your teeth.

YOU CAN CATCH POISON IVY FROM THE AIR ?

SENSE

You can get poison ivy only by coming in contact with the oily substance found in poison ivy plants. But if poison ivy plants are burned, oil droplets can travel on floating ash or soot. If the ash settles on your skin, you may very well get poison ivy.

You can even get poison ivy by touching the clothes of someone who has come in contact with the plant. The oil can stick to clothes, to shoes, to a stick, to a bicycle, even to a dog or cat. If you are sensitive to poison ivy and touch something that has touched the plant, you can easily come down with a poison-ivy rash.

The easiest way to recognize a poison-ivy plant is by remembering the old rhyme, "Leaves of three,/Let them be." Poison-ivy leaves are usually shiny green with saw-tooth edges. But they can be a different color in autumn and have a different look in different places. But the one thing that never changes is the grouping of three leaves on each stem. So if you find a plant with three leaves, don't touch it.

READING IN BED CAN RUIN YOUR EYES ?

NONSENSE

Reading in bed will not harm your eyes. But it is not the easiest position for your eye muscles. Your eyes will become tired sooner than if you read sitting up.

With enough light, your eyes can adjust to seeing in any position. Your eye muscles move and focus your eyes. Just as your arm or leg muscles can tire, so can your eye muscles tire. When you read in a strained position, your eye muscles tire and start to ache. Resting your eyes will stop them from aching.

The most comfortable position for your eye muscles is to sit up straight in a chair or in bed. Then the muscles will not be under strain and will not ache.

Reading in a moving car also tires your eye muscles. That's because the letters keep jumping around as the car moves. Reading the letters means constantly moving your eyes. That can strain the muscles and even give you a headache. But it will not ruin your eyes.